A BOOK

By WILLIAM ERNEST HENLEY

1893

Fourth Edition

Copyright © 2011 Read Books Ltd.
This book is copyright and may not be
reproduced or copied in any way without
the express permission of the publisher in writing

British Library Cataloguing-in-Publication Data
A catalogue record for this book is available from
the British Library

William Ernest Henley

William Ernest Henley was born on 23rd August 1849, in Gloucester, England.

He attended Crypt Grammar School in Gloucester where the poet, scholar, and theologian, T. E. Brown, was headmaster. Brown had a made a huge impression on the young Henley and the two struck up a lifelong friendship. Henley claimed Brown to be "a man of Genius – the first I'd ever seen", and upon Brown's death in 1897, Henley wrote an admiring obituary to him in the *New Review*.

From the age of 12, Henley suffered from tuberculosis of the bone which eventually resulted in his left leg having to be amputated below the knee. According to Robert Louis Stevenson's letters, the character of Long John Silver was inspired by his friend Henley.

In 1867, Henley passed the Oxford Local Schools

Examination and set off to London to establish himself as a journalist. Unfortunately, his career was frequently interrupted by long stays in hospital due to a diseased right foot which he refused to have amputated. During a three year stay at the Royal Infirmary of Edinburgh, Henley wrote and published his collection of poetry *In Hospital* (1875). This publication is noteworthy in particular for being some of the earliest examples of free verse written in England.

Henley married Hannah (Anna) Johnson Boyle on 22nd January 1878. The couple had one daughter together, Margaret, who died at the age of five and is reportedly the source of the name Wendy in J. M. Barrie's *Peter Pan*. Apparently she used to call Barrie her "fwendy wendy", resulting in the use of the name in the children's classic.

Henley's best-remembered work is his poem "Invictus", written in 1888. It is a passionate and defiant poem, reportedly written as a demonstration of resilience following the amputation of his leg. This poem was famously recited to fellow inmates at Robben Island prison by Nelson Mandela to spread the message of empowerment and self-mastery. He also wrote a notable work of literary criticisms, *Views and Reviews,* in 1890, in which he covered a wide range of works by prominent authors.

Henley died of tuberculosis in 1903 at the age of 53 at his home in Woking, and his ashes were interred in his daughter's grave in the churchyard at Cockayne Hatley in Bedfordshire, England.

TO MY WIFE

Take, dear, my little sheaf of songs,
　　For, old or new,
All that is good in them belongs
　　Only to you;

And, singing as when all was young,
　　They will recall
Those others, lived but left unsung—
　　The best of all.

　　　　　　　　　W. E. H.

APRIL 1888

CONTENTS

IN HOSPITAL: RHYMES AND RHYTHMS

		PAGE
I.	Enter Patient	3
II.	Waiting	4
III.	Interior	5
IV.	Before	7
V.	Operation	8
VI.	After	10
VII.	Vigil	11
VIII.	Staff-Nurse: Old Style	14
IX.	Lady-Probationer	15
X.	Staff-Nurse: New Style	16
XI.	Clinical	17
XII.	Etching	20
XIII.	Casualty	22
XIV.	Ave, Caesar!	24
XV.	'The Chief'	26
XVI.	House-Surgeon	27

CONTENTS

In Hospital: Rhymes and Rhythms—continued

		PAGE
XVII.	Interlude	28
XVIII.	Children: Private Ward	30
XIX.	Scrubber	31
XX.	Visitor	32
XXI.	Romance	33
XXII.	Pastoral	35
XXIII.	Music	37
XXIV.	Suicide	39
XXV.	Apparition	41
XXVI.	Anterotics	42
XXVII.	Nocturn	43
XXVIII.	Discharged	45
Envoy		47

LIFE AND DEATH (ECHOES)

I.	Chiming a dream by the way	51
II.	Life is bitter	53
III.	O gather me the rose	54
IV.	Out of the night that covers me	56
V.	I am the Reaper	58
VI.	Praise the generous gods	60
VII.	Fill a glass with golden wine	61
VIII.	In the time of snows	62

CONTENTS

Life and Death (Echoes)—continued

		PAGE
IX.	We'll go no more a-roving	64
X.	The sea is full of wandering foam	65
XI.	Thick is the darkness	66
XII.	To me at my fifth-floor window	67
XIII.	Bring her again, O western wind	68
XIV.	The wan sun westers faint and slow	69
XV.	There is a wheel inside my head	71
XVI.	While the west is paling	72
XVII.	The sands are alive with sunshine	73
XVIII.	The nightingale has a lyre of gold	74
XIX.	Your heart has trembled to my tongue	75
XX.	The surges gushed and sounded	76
XXI.	We flash across the level	77
XXII.	The West a glimmering lake of light	79
XXIII.	The skies are strown with stars	81
XXIV.	The full sea rolls and thunders	82
XXV.	In the year that's come and gone	83
XXVI.	She sauntered by the swinging seas	85
XXVII.	Blithe dreams arise to greet us	86
XXVIII.	A Child	89
XXIX.	Kate-a-Whimsies, John-a-Dreams	91
XXX.	The pretty washermaiden	92
XXXI.	O Falmouth is a fine town	93
XXXII.	The ways are green	95
XXXIII.	Life in her creaking shoes	97

Life and Death (Echoes)—continued

		PAGE
XXXIV.	A late lark twitters from the quiet skies	99
XXXV.	Or ever the knightly years were gone	101
XXXVI.	On the way to Kew	103
XXXVII.	The past was goodly once	105
XXXVIII.	The spring, my dear	106
XXXIX.	The Spirit of Wine	107
XL.	A wink from Hesper	110
XLI.	Friends . . . old friends . . .	111
XLII.	If it should come to be	113
XLIII.	From the brake the Nightingale	114
XLIV.	In the waste hour	116
XLV.	Crosses and troubles	119

BRIC-À-BRAC

BALLADES

Of a Toyokuni Colour-Print	123
Of Youth and Age	125
Of the Frowardness of Woman	127
Of Rain	129
Of Antique Dances	132
Of Spring Music	134
Of Midsummer Days and Nights	136
Of Dead Actors	138
Made in the Hot Weather	140

CONTENTS

BALLADS—*continued*

	PAGE
Of June	143
Of Ladies' Names	145
Of Life and Fate	147

RONDELS

I. In the street of By-and-By	150
II. Felicity: Enquire Within	151
III. We'll to the woods and gather may	152
IV. Beside the idle summer sea	153
V. The ways of Death are soothing and serene	154
VI. We shall surely die	155

SONNETS AND QUATORZAINS

At Queensferry	156
Orientale	157
Forenoon	158
In Fisherrow	159
Rain	160
Back-View	161
Croquis	162
Jenny Wren	163
Attadale, West Highlands	164
From a Window in Princes Street	165
In the Dials	166

RONDEAUS

		PAGE
I.	My love to me	167
II.	With strawberries	168
III.	The leaves are sere	169
IV.	Let us be drunk	170
V.	If I were king	171
VI.	When you are old	172
VII.	What is to come	174

IN HOSPITAL

RHYMES
AND
RHYTHMS

On ne saurait dire à quel point un homme, seul dans son lit et malade, devient personnel.—BALZAC.

I

ENTER PATIENT

THE morning mists still haunt the stony street;
　　The northern summer air is shrill and cold;
And lo, the Hospital, gray, quiet, old,
Where life and death like friendly chafferers meet.
Thro' the loud spaciousness and draughty gloom
A small, strange child—so agèd yet so young!—
Her little arm besplinted and beslung,
Precedes me gravely to the waiting room.
I limp behind, my confidence all gone.
The gray-haired soldier-porter waves me on,
And on I crawl, and still my spirits fail:
A tragic meanness seems so to environ
These corridors and stairs of stone and iron,
Cold, naked, clean—half-workhouse and half-jail.

II

WAITING

A SQUARE, squat room (a cellar on promotion),
    Drab to the soul, drab to the very daylight;
Plasters astray in unnatural-looking tinware;
Scissors and lint and apothecary's jars.

Here, on a bench a skeleton would writhe from,
    Angry and sore, I wait to be admitted:
Wait till my heart is lead upon my stomach,
While at their ease two dressers do their chores.

One has a probe—it feels to me a crowbar.
    A small boy sniffs and shudders after bluestone.
A poor old tramp explains his poor old ulcers.
Life is (I think) a blunder and a shame.

III

INTERIOR

THE gaunt brown walls
    Look infinite in their decent meanness.
There is nothing of home in the noisy kettle,
    The fulsome fire.

    The atmosphere
Suggests the trail of a ghostly druggist.
Dressings and lint on the long, lean table—
    Whom are they for?

    The patients yawn,
Or lie as in training for shroud and coffin.
A nurse in the corridor scolds and wrangles.
    It's grim and strange.

Far footfalls clank.
The bad burn waits with his head unbandaged.
My neighbour chokes in the clutch of chloral . . .
O a gruesome world!

IV

BEFORE

BEHOLD me waiting—waiting for the knife.
    A little while, and at a leap I storm
The thick, sweet mystery of chloroform,
The drunken dark, the little death-in-life.
The gods are good to me: I have no wife,
No innocent child, to think of as I near
The fateful minute; nothing all-too dear
Unmans me for my bout of passive strife.
Yet am I tremulous and a trifle sick,
And, face to face with chance, I shrink a little:
My hopes are strong, my will is something weak.
Here comes the basket? Thank you. I am ready.
But, gentlemen my porters, life is brittle:
You carry Cæsar and his fortunes—steady!

v

OPERATION

YOU are carried in a basket,
    Like a carcase from the shambles,
To the theatre, a cockpit
Where they stretch you on a table.

Then they bid you close your eyelids,
    And they mask you with a napkin,
And the anæsthetic reaches
Hot and subtle through your being.

And you gasp and reel and shudder
    In a rushing, swaying rapture,
While the voices at your elbow
Fade—receding—fainter—farther.

Lights about you shower and tumble,
    And your blood seems crystallising—
    Edged and vibrant, yet within you
    Racked and hurried back and forward.

Then the lights grow fast and furious,
    And you hear a noise of waters,
    And you wrestle, blind and dizzy,
    In an agony of effort,

Till a sudden lull accepts you,
    And you sound an utter darkness . . .
    And awaken . . . with a struggle . . .
    On a hushed, attentive audience.

VI

AFTER

LIKEAS a flamelet blanketed in smoke,
    So through the anæsthetic shows my life;
So flashes and so fades my thought, at strife
With the strong stupor that I heave and choke
And sicken at, it is so foully sweet.
Faces look strange from space—and disappear.
Far voices, sudden loud, offend my ear—
And hush as sudden. Then my senses fleet:
All were a blank, save for this dull, new pain
That grinds my leg and foot; and brokenly
Time and the place glimpse on to me again;
And, unsurprised, out of uncertainty,
I wake—relapsing—somewhat faint and fain,
To an immense, complacent dreamery.

VII

VIGIL

L IVED on one's back,
  In the long hours of repose
Life is a practical nightmare—
Hideous asleep or awake. ·

Shoulders and loins
Ache - - - !
Ache, and the mattress,
Run into boulders and hummocks,
Glows like a kiln, while the bedclothes—
Tumbling, importunate, daft—
Ramble and roll, and the gas,
Screwed to its lowermost,
An inevitable atom of light,

Haunts, and a stertorous sleeper
Snores me to hate and despair.

All the old time
Surges malignant before me;
Old voices, old kisses, old songs
Blossom derisive about me;
While the new days
Pass me in endless procession:
A pageant of shadows
Silently, leeringly wending
On . . . and still on . . . still on.

Far in the stillness a cat
Languishes loudly. A cinder
Falls, and the shadows
Lurch to the leap of the flame. The next man to me
Turns with a moan; and the snorer,
The drug like a rope at his throat,
Gasps, gurgles, snorts himself free, as the night-nurse,
Noiseless and strange,

Her bull's-eye half-lanterned in apron,
(Whispering me, 'Are ye no sleepin' yet?')
Passes, list-slippered and peering,
Round . . . and is gone.

Sleep comes at last—
Sleep full of dreams and misgivings—
Broken with brutal and sordid
Voices and sounds that impose on me,
Ere I can wake to it,
The unnatural, intolerable day.

.

VIII

STAFF-NURSE: OLD STYLE

THE greater masters of the commonplace,
    REMBRANDT and good SIR WALTER—only these
Could paint her all to you: experienced ease
And antique liveliness and ponderous grace;
The sweet old roses of her sunken face;
The depth and malice of her sly gray eyes;
The broad Scots tongue that flatters, scolds, defies;
The thick Scots wit that fells you like a mace.
These thirty years has she been nursing here,
Some of them under SYME, her hero still.
Much is she worth, and even more is made of her.
Patients and students hold her very dear.
The doctors love her, tease her, use her skill.
They say 'The Chief' himself is half-afraid of her.

IX

LADY-PROBATIONER

SOME three, or five, or seven, and thirty years;
    A Roman nose; a dimpling double-chin;
Dark eyes and shy that, ignorant of sin,
Are yet acquainted, it would seem, with tears;
A comely shape; a slim, high-coloured hand,
Graced, rather oddly, with a signet ring;
A bashful air, becoming everything;
A well-bred silence always at command.
Her plain print gown, prim cap, and bright steel chain
Look out of place on her, and I remain
Absorbed in her, as in a pleasant mystery. ·
Quick, skilful, quiet, soft in speech and touch . . .
'Do you like nursing?' 'Yes, Sir, very much.'
Somehow, I rather think she has a history.

X

STAFF-NURSE: NEW STYLE

BLUE-eyed and bright of face but waning fast
    Into the sere of virginal decay,
I view her as she enters, day by day,
As a sweet sunset almost overpast.
Kindly and calm, patrician to the last,
Superbly falls her gown of sober gray,
And on her chignon's elegant array
The plainest cap is somehow touched with caste.
She talks BEETHOVEN; frowns disapprobation
At BALZAC's name, sighs it at 'poor GEORGE SAND's';
Knows that she has exceeding pretty hands;
Speaks Latin with a right accentuation;
And gives at need (as one who understands)
Draught, counsel, diagnosis, exhortation.

XI

CLINICAL

Hist? . . .
    Through the corridor's echoes
Louder and nearer
Comes a great shuffling of feet.
Quick, every one of you,
Straighten your quilts, and be decent!
Here's the Professor.

In he comes first
With the bright look we know,
From the broad, white brows the kind eyes
Soothing yet nerving you.   Here, at his elbow,
White-capped, white-aproned, the Nurse,
Towel on arm and her inkstand
Fretful with quills.

Here, in the ruck, anyhow,
Surging along,
Louts, duffers, exquisites, students, and prigs—
Whiskers and foreheads, scarf-pins and spectacles—
Hustle the Class! And they ring themselves
Round the first bed, where the Chief
(His dressers and clerks at attention)
Bends in inspection already.

So shows the ring
Seen from behind round a conjuror
Doing his pitch in the street.
High shoulders, low shoulders, broad shoulders,
    narrow ones,
Round, square, and angular, serry and shove;
While from within a voice,
Gravely and weightily fluent,
Sounds; and then ceases; and suddenly
(Look at the stress of the shoulders!)
Out of a quiver of silence,
Over the hiss of the spray,
Comes a low cry, and the sound

Of breath quick intaken through teeth
Clenched in resolve. And the Master
Breaks from the crowd, and goes,
Wiping his hands,
To the next bed, with his pupils
Flocking and whispering behind him.

Now one can see.
Case Number One
Sits (rather pale) with his bed-clothes
Stripped up, and showing his foot
(Alas for God's image!)
Swaddled in wet, white lint
Brilliantly hideous with red.

XII

ETCHING

TWO and thirty is the ploughman.
    He's a man of gallant inches,
And his hair is close and curly,
    And his beard;
But his face is wan and sunken,
And his eyes are large and brilliant,
And his shoulder-blades are sharp,
    And his knees.

He is weak of wits, religious,
Full of sentiment and yearning,
Gentle, faded—with a cough
    And a snore.
When his wife (who was a widow,
And is many years his elder)
Fails to write, and that is always,
    He desponds.

Let his melancholy wander,
And he'll tell you pretty stories
Of the women that have wooed him
 Long ago;
Or he'll sing of bonnie lasses
Keeping sheep among the heather,
With a crackling, hackling click
 In his voice.

XIII

CASUALTY

As with varnish red and glistening
    Dripped his hair; his feet were rigid;
Raised, he settled stiffly sideways:
You could see the hurts were spinal.

He had fallen from an engine,
    And been dragged along the metals.
    It was hopeless, and they knew it;
    So they covered him, and left him.

As he lay, by fits half sentient,
    Inarticulately moaning,
    With his stockinged feet protruded
    Stark and awkward from the blankets,

To his bed there came a woman,
  Stood and looked and sighed a little,
  And departed without speaking,
  As himself a few hours after.

I was told it was his sweetheart.
  They were on the eve of marriage.
  She was quiet as a statue,
  But her lip was gray and writhen.

XIV

AVE, CAESAR!

FROM the winter's gray despair,
    From the summer's golden languor,
Death, the lover of Life,
Frees us for ever.

Inevitable, silent, unseen,
Everywhere always,
Shadow by night and as light in the day,
Signs she at last to her chosen;
And, as she waves them forth,
Sorrow and Joy
Lay by their looks and their voices,
Set down their hopes, and are made
One in the dim Forever.

Into the winter's gray delight,

Into the summer's golden dream,
Holy and high and impartial,
Death, the mother of Life,
Mingles all men for ever.

XV

'THE CHIEF'

HIS brow spreads large and placid, and his eye
   Is deep and bright, with steady looks that still
Soft lines of tranquil thought his face fulfill—
His face at once benign and proud and shy.
If envy scout, if ignorance deny,
His faultless patience, his unyielding will,
Beautiful gentleness, and splendid skill,
Innumerable gratitudes reply.
His wise, rare smile is sweet with certainties,
And seems in all his patients to compel
Such love and faith as failure cannot quell.
We hold him for another Herakles,
Battling with custom, prejudice, disease,
As once the son of Zeus with Death and Hell.

XVI

HOUSE-SURGEON

EXCEEDING tall, but built so well his height
   Half-disappears in flow of chest and limb
Moustache and whisker trooper-like in trim;
Frank-faced, frank-eyed, frank-hearted; always bright
And always punctual—morning, noon, and night;
Bland as a Jesuit, sober as a hymn;
Humorous, and yet without a touch of whim;
Gentle and amiable, yet full of fight;
His piety, though fresh and true in strain,
Has not yet whitewashed up his common mood
To the dead blank of his particular Schism:
Sweet, unaggressive, tolerant, most humane,
Wild artists like his kindly elderhood,
And cultivate his mild Philistinism.

XVII

INTERLUDE

O THE fun, the fun and frolic
    That *The Wind that Shakes the Barley*
Scatters through a penny whistle
Tickled with artistic fingers !

Kate the scrubber (forty summers,
    Stout but sportive) treads a measure,
Grinning, in herself a ballet,
Fixed as fate upon her audience.

Stumps are shaking, crutch-supported ;
    Splinted fingers tap the rhythm ;
And a head all helmed with plasters
Wags a measured approbation.

Of their mattress-life oblivious,
   All the patients, brisk and cheerful,
   Are encouraging the dancer,
   And applauding the musician.

Dim the gases in the output
   Of so many ardent smokers,
   Full of shadow lurch the corners,
   And the doctor peeps and passes.

There are, maybe, some suspicions
   Of an alcoholic presence . . .
   'Tak' a sup of this, my wumman!' . . .
   New Year comes but once a twelvemonth.

XVIII

CHILDREN: PRIVATE WARD

HERE in this dim, dull, double-bedded room,
    I am a father to a brace of boys,
Ailing but apt for every sort of noise,
Bedfast but brilliant yet with health and bloom.
Roden, the Irishman, is 'sieven past,'
Blue-eyed, snub-nosed, chubby, and fair of face.
Willie's but six, and seems to like the place,
A cheerful little collier to the last.
They eat, and laugh, and sing, and fight, all day;
All night they sleep like dormice. See them play
At Operations:—Roden, the Professor,
Saws, lectures, takes the artery up, and ties;
Willie, self-chloroformed, with half-shut eyes,
Holding the limb and moaning—Case and Dresser.

XIX

SCRUBBER

SHE's tall and gaunt, and in her hard, sad face
  With flashes of the old fun's animation
There lowers the fixed and peevish resignation
Bred of a past where troubles came apace.
She tells me that her husband, ere he died,
Saw seven of their children pass away,
And never knew the little lass at play
Out on the green, in whom he's deified.
Her kin dispersed, her friends forgot and gone,
All simple faith her honest Irish mind,
Scolding her spoiled young saint, she labours on:
Telling her dreams, taking her patients' part,
Trailing her coat sometimes: and you shall find
No rougher, quainter speech, nor kinder heart.

XX

VISITOR

HER little face is like a walnut shell
    With wrinkling lines; her soft, white hair adorns
Her either brow in quaint, straight curls, like horns;
And all about her clings an old, sweet smell.
Prim is her gown and quakerlike her shawl.
Well might her bonnets have been born on her.
Can you conceive a Fairy Godmother
The subject of a real religious call?
In snow or shine, from bed to bed she runs,
Her mittened hands, that ever give or pray,
Bearing a sheaf of tracts, a bag of buns,
All twinkling smiles and texts and pious tales:
A wee old maid that sweeps the Bridegroom's way,
Strong in a cheerful trust that never fails.

XXI

ROMANCE

'TALK of pluck!' pursued the Sailor,
    Set at euchre on his elbow,
'I was on the wharf at Charleston,
Just ashore from off the runner.

'It was gray and dirty weather,
    And I heard a drum go rolling,
Rub-a-dubbing in the distance,
Awful dour-like and defiant.

'In and out among the cotton,
    Mud, and chains, and stores, and anchors,
Tramped a squad of battered scarecrows—
Poor old Dixie's bottom dollar!

'Some hád shoes, but all had rifles,
  Them that wasn't bald was beardless,
  And the drum was rolling *Dixie*,
  And they stepped to it like men, sir!

'Rags and tatters, belts and bayonets,
  On they swung, the drum a-rolling,
  Mum and sour. It looked like fighting,
  And they meant it too, by thunder!'

XXII

PASTORAL

IT'S the Spring.
   Earth has conceived, and her bosom,
Teeming with summer, is glad.

Thro' the green land,
Vistas of change and adventure,
The gray roads go beckoning and winding,
Peopled with wains, and melodious
With harness-bells jangling,
Jangling and twangling rough rhythms
To the slow march of the stately, great horses
Whistled and shouted along.

White fleets of cloud,
Argosies heavy with fruitfulness,
Sail the blue peacefully. Green flame the hedgerows.

Blackbirds are bugling, and white in wet winds
Sway the tall poplars.
Pageants of colour and fragrance,
Pass the sweet meadows, and viewless
Walks the mild spirit of May,
Visibly blessing the world.

O the brilliance of blossoming orchards!
O the savour and thrill of the woods,
When their leafage is stirred
By the flight of the angel of rain!
Loud lows the steer; in the fallows
Rooks are alert; and the brooks
Gurgle and tinkle and trill. Thro' the gloaming,
Under the rare, shy stars,
Boy and girl wander
Dreaming in darkness and dew.

It's the Spring.
A sprightliness feeble and squalid
Wakes in the ward, and I sicken,
Impotent, winter at heart.

XXIII

MUSIC

Down the quiet eve,
    Thro' my window with the sunset
Pipes to me a distant organ
Foolish ditties;

And, as when you change
Pictures in a magic lantern,
Books, beds, bottles, floor, and ceiling
Fade and vanish,

And I'm well once more. . . .
August flares adust and torrid,
But my heart is full of April
Sap and sweetness.

In the quiet eve
I am loitering, longing, dreaming . . . .
Dreaming, and a distant organ
Pipes me ditties.

I can see the shop,
I can smell the sprinkled pavement,
Where she serves—her chestnut chignon
Thrills my senses.

O the sight and scent,
Wistful eve and perfumed pavement!
In the distance pipes an organ . . .
The sensation

Comes tó me anew,
And my spirit for a moment
Thro' the music breathes the blessèd
Air of London.

XXIV

SUICIDE

STARING corpselike at the ceiling,
    See the harsh, unrazored features,
Ghastly brown against his pillow,
And the throat—so strangely bandaged!

Lack of work and lack of victuals,
    A debauch of smuggled whisky,
And his children in the workhouse
Made the world so black a riddle

That he plunged for a solution;
    And, although his knife was edgeless,
He was sinking fast towards one,
When they came and found and saved him.

Stupid now with shame and sorrow,
In the night I hear him sobbing.
But sometimes he talks a little.
He has told me all his troubles.

In his face, so tanned and bloodless,
White and wide his eyeballs glitter;
And his smile, occult and tragic,
Makes you shudder when you see it.

XXV

APPARITION

THIN-legged, thin-chested, slight unspeakably,
 Neat-footed and weak-fingered: in his face—
Lean, large-boned, curved of beak, and touched with race,
Bold-lipped, rich-tinted, mutable as the sea,
The brown eyes radiant with vivacity—
There shines a brilliant and romantic grace,
A spirit intense and rare, with trace on trace
Of passion and impudence and energy.
Valiant in velvet, light in ragged luck,
Most vain, most generous, sternly critical,
Buffoon and poet, lover and sensualist:
A deal of Ariel, just a streak of Puck,
Much Antony, of Hamlet most of all,
And something of the Shorter-Catechist.

XXVI

ANTEROTICS

LAUGHS the happy April morn
    Thro' my grimy, little window,
And a shaft of sunshine pushes
Thro' the shadows in the square.

Dogs are romping thro' the grass,
    Crows are cawing round the chimneys,
And among the bleaching linen
Goes the west at hide-and-seek.

Loud and cheerful clangs the bell.
    Here the nurses troop to breakfast.
Handsome, ugly, all are women . . .
O the Spring—the Spring—the Spring!

XXVII

NOCTURN

AT the barren heart of midnight,
    When the shadow shuts and opens
As the loud flames pulse and flutter,
I can hear a cistern leaking.

Dripping, dropping, in a rhythm,
    Rough, unequal, half-melodious,
Like the measures aped from nature
In the infancy of music;

Like the buzzing of an insect,
    Still, irrational, persistent, . . .
I must listen, listen, listen
In a passion of attention;

Till it taps upon my heartstrings,
And my very life goes dripping,
Dropping, dripping, drip-drip-dropping,
In the drip-drop of the cistern.

XXVIII

DISCHARGED

CARRY me out
  Into the wind and the sunshine,
Into the beautiful world.

O the wonder, the spell of the streets!
The stature and strength of the horses,
The rustle and echo of footfalls,
The flat roar and rattle of wheels!
A swift tram floats huge on us . . .
It's a dream?
The smell of the mud in my nostrils
Blows brave—like a breath of the sea!

As of old,
Ambulant, undulant drapery,

Vaguely and strangely provocative,
Flutters and beckons. O yonder—
Scarlet !—the glint of a stocking !
Sudden a spire
Wedged in the mist ! O the houses,
The long lines of lofty, gray houses,
Cross-hatched with shadow and light !
These are the streets. . . .
Each is an avenue leading
Whither I will !

Free . . . !
Dizzy, hysterical, faint,
I sit, and the carriage rolls on with me
Into the wonderful world.

THE OLD INFIRMARY EDINBURGH 1873-75

ENVOY

To Charles Baxter

DO you remember
    That afternoon—that Sunday afternoon!—
When, as the kirks were ringing in
And the gray city teemed
With Sabbath feelings and aspects,
LEWIS—our LEWIS then,
Now the whole world's—and you,
Young, yet in shape most like an elder, came,
Laden with BALZACS
(Big, yellow books, quite impudently French),
The first of many times
To that transformed back-kitchen where I lay
So long, so many centuries—
Or years is it!—ago?

Dear CHARLES, since then

We have been friends, LEWIS and you and I,
(How good it sounds, 'LEWIS and you and I!'):
Such friends, I like to think,
That in us three, LEWIS and me and you,
Is something of that gallant dream
Which old DUMAS—the generous, the humane,
The seven-and-seventy times to be forgiven!—
Dreamed for a blessing to the race,
The immortal *Musketeers*.

Our ATHOS rests—the wise, the kind,
The liberal and august, his fault atoned,
Rests in the crowded yard
There at the west of Princes Street. We three—
You, I, and LEWIS!—still afoot,
Are still together, and our lives,
In chime so long, may keep
(God bless the thought!)
Unjangled till the end.
W. E. H.

CHISWICK *March* 1888

LIFE AND DEATH
(ECHOES)

Aquì esta encerrada el alma del licenciado Pedro Garcìas.
GIL BLAS *AU LECTEUR*

I

TO MY MOTHER

CHIMING a dream by the way
  With ocean's rapture and roar,
I met a maiden to-day
  Walking alone on the shore:
Walking in maiden wise,
  Modest and kind and fair,
The freshness of spring in her eyes
  And the fulness of spring in her hair.

Cloud-shadow and scudding sun-burst
  Were swift on the floor of the sea,
And a mad wind was romping its worst,
  But what was their magic to me?

What the charm of the midsummer skies?
  I only saw she was there,
A dream of the sea in her eyes
  And the kiss of the sea in her hair.

I watched her vanish in space;
  She came where I walked no more;
But something had passed of her grace
  To the spell of the wave and the shore;
And now, as the glad stars rise,
  She comes to me rosy and rare,
The delight of the wind in her eyes
  And the hand of the wind in her hair.

1872

II

LIFE is bitter. All the faces of the years,
  Young and old, are gray with travail and with tears.
Must we only wake to toil, to tire, to weep?
In the sun, among the leaves, upon the flowers,
Slumber stills to dreamy death the heavy hours . . .
  Let me sleep.

Riches won but mock the old unable years;
Fame's a pearl that hides beneath a sea of tears;
  Love must wither, or must live alone and weep.
In the sun, between the leaves, across the flowers,
While we slumber, death approaches through the hours . . .
  Let me sleep.

1872

III

O GATHER me the rose, the rose,
    While yet in flower we find it,
For summer smiles, but summer goes,
    And winter waits behind it.

For with the dream foregone, foregone,
    The deed forborne for ever,
The worm, regret, will canker on,
    And time will turn him never.

So well it were to love, my love,
    And cheat of any laughter
The fate beneath us and above,
    The dark before and after.

The myrtle and the rose, the rose,
    The sunshine and the swallow,
The dream that comes, the wish that goes,
    The memories that follow!

1874

IV

To R. T. H. B.

Out of the night that covers me,
    Black as the pit from pole to pole,
I thank whatever gods may be
    For my unconquerable soul.

In the fell clutch of circumstance
    I have not winced nor cried aloud.
Under the bludgeonings of chance
    My head is bloody, but unbowed.

Beyond this place of wrath and tears
    Looms but the Horror of the shade,
And yet the menace of the years
    Finds and shall find me unafraid.

It matters not how strait the gate,
  How charged with punishments the scroll,
I am the master of my fate:
  I am the captain of my soul.

1875

V

I AM the Reaper.
　All things with heedful hook
Silent I gather.
Pale roses touched with the spring,
Tall corn in summer,
Fruits rich with autumn, and frail winter blossoms—
Reaping, still reaping—
All things with heedful hook
Timely I gather.

I am the Sower.
All the unbodied life
Runs through my seed-sheet.
Atom with atom wed,
Each quickening the other,
Fall through my hands, ever changing, still changeless.

Ceaselessly sowing,
Life, incorruptible life,
Flows from my seed-sheet.

Maker and breaker,
I am the ebb and the flood,
Here and Hereafter.
Sped through the tangle and coil
Of infinite nature,
Viewless and soundless I fashion all being.
Taker and giver,
I am the womb and the grave,
The Now and the Ever.

1875

VI

PRAISE the generous gods for giving
    In a world of wrath and strife
With a little time for living
    Unto all the joy of life.

At whatever source we drink it,
    Art or love or faith or wine,
In whatever terms we think it,
    It is common and divine.

Praise the high gods, for in giving
    This to man, and this alone,
They have made his chance of living
    Shine the equal of their own.

1875

VII

FILL a glass with golden wine,
    And the while your lips are wet
Set their perfume unto mine,
    And forget
Every kiss we take and give
Leaves us less of life to live.

Yet again! Your whim and mine
    In a happy while have met.
All your sweets to me resign,
    Nor regret
That we press with every breath,
Sighed or singing, nearer death.

1875

VIII

IN the time of snows
   A thought that glows
And a hope that follows fearless.
  In the time of buds
   Two beating bloods
And an impulse blind and careless.

In the time of leaves
   A heart that heaves
And a heart that dreads the morrow.
  In the time of fruit
   A wandering foot
And afar a lonely sorrow.

This is the use
Of them that loose
Their sail to the wind of pleasure:
　The year outrun,
　The dream undone,
And the long, regretful leisure.

1875

IX

WE'll go no more a-roving by the light of the moon.
    November glooms are barren beside the dusk of June.
The summer flowers are faded, the summer thoughts
    are sere :
We'll go no more a-roving, lest worse befall, my dear.

We'll go no more a-roving by the light of the moon.
The song we sang rings hollow, and heavy runs the tune.
Glad ways and words remembered would shame the
    wretched year.
We'll go no more a-roving, nor dream we did, my dear.

We'll go no more a-roving by the light of the moon.
If yet we walk together, we need not shun the noon.
No sweet thing left to savour, no sad thing left to fear,
We'll go no more a-roving, but weep at home, my dear.

                                        1875

X

THE sea is full of wandering foam,
    The sky of driving cloud;
My restless thoughts among them roam . . .
    The night is dark and loud.

Where are the hours that came to me
    So beautiful and bright?
A wild wind shakes the wilder sea . . .
    O dark and loud's the night!

1876

XI

THICK is the darkness—
    Sunward, O sunward!
Rough is the highway—
    Onward, still onward!

Dawn harbours surely
    East of the shadows.
Facing us somewhere
    Spread the sweet meadows.

Upward and forward!
    Time will restore us:
Light is above us,
    Rest is before us.

1876

XII

TO me at my fifth-floor window
    The chimney-pots in rows
Are sets of pipes pandean
    For every wind that blows;

And the smoke that whirls and eddies
    In a thousand times and keys
Is really a visible music
    Set to my reveries.

O monstrous pipes, melodious
    With fitful tune and dream,
The clouds are your only audience,
    Her thought is your only theme!

1875

XIII

BRING her again, O western wind,
    Over the western sea:
Gentle and good and fair and kind,
    Bring her again to me.

Not that her fancy holds me dear,
    Not that a hope may be:
Only that I may know her near,
    Wind of the western sea.

1875

XIV

THE wan sun westers faint and slow;
    The eastern distance glimmers gray;
An eerie haze comes creeping low
    Across the little, lonely bay;
    And from the sky-line far away
About the quiet heaven are spread
    Mysterious hints of dying day,
Thin, delicate dreams of green and red.

And weak, reluctant surges lap
    And rustle round and down the strand.
No other sound . . . . If it should hap,
    The ship that sails from fairy-land!
    The silken shrouds with spells are manned,
The hull is magically scrolled,
    The squat mast lives, and in the sand
The gold prow-griffin claws a hold.

It steals to sea-ward silently;
  Strange fish-folk follow thro' the gloom;
Great wings flap overhead; I see
  The Castle of the Drowsy Doom
  Vague thro' the changeless twilight loom,
Enchanted, hushed. And ever there
  She slumbers in eternal bloom,
Her cushions hid with golden hair.

1875

XV

THERE is a wheel inside my head
   Of wantonness and wine,
  A cracked old fiddle is grunting without;
But the wind with scents of the sea is fed,
   And the sun seems glad to shine.

The sun and the wind are akin to you,
   As you are akin to June;
     But the fiddle! . . . it giggles and buzzes about,
And, love and laughter! who gave him the cue?—
   He's playing your favourite tune.

1875

XVI

WHILE the west is paling
    Starshine is begun.
While the dusk is failing
    Glimmers up the sun.

So, till darkness cover
    Life's retreating gleam,
Lover follows lover,
    Dream succeeds to dream.

Stoop to my endeavour,
    O my love, and be
Only and for ever
    Sun and stars to me.

1876

XVII

THE sands are alive with sunshine,
    The bathers lounge and throng,
And out in the bay a bugle
    Is lilting a gallant song.

The clouds go racing eastward,
    The blithe wind cannot rest,
And a shard on the shingle flashes,
    Like the shining soul of a jest.

While children romp in the surges,
    And sweethearts wander free,
And the Firth as with laughter dimples . . .
    I would it were deep over me!

1875

XVIII

THE nightingale has a lyre of gold,
    The lark's is a clarion call,
And the blackbird plays but a box-wood flute,
    But I love him best of all.

For his song is all of the joy of life,
    And we in the mad spring weather,
We two have listened till he sang
    Our hearts and lips together.

1876

XIX

YOUR heart has trembled to my tongue,
    Your hands in mine have lain,
Your thought to me has leaned and clung,
    Again and yet again,
      My dear,
    Again and yet again.

Now die the dream, or come the wife,
    The past is not in vain,
For wholly as it was your life
    Can never be again,
      My dear,
    Can never be again.

1876

XX

THE surges gushed and sounded,
  The blue was the blue of June,
And low above the brightening east
  Floated a shred of moon.

The woods were black and solemn,
  The night winds large and free,
And in your thought a blessing seemed
  To fall on land and sea.

1877

XXI

WE flash across the level.
    We thunder thro' the bridges.
We bicker down the cuttings.
    We sway along the ridges.

A rush of streaming hedges,
    Of jostling lights and shadows,
Of hurtling, hurrying stations,
    Of racing woods and meadows.

We charge the tunnels headlong—
    The blackness roars and shatters.
We crash between embankments—
    The open spins and scatters.

We shake off the miles like water,
We might carry a royal ransom;
And I think of her waiting, waiting,
And long for a common hansom.

1876

XXII

THE West a glimmering lake of light,
    A dream of pearly weather,
The first of stars is burning white—
    The star we watch together.
Is April dead? The unresting year
    Will shape us our September,
And April's work is done, my dear—
    Do you not remember?

O gracious eve! O happy star,
    Still-flashing, glowing, sinking!—
Who lives of lovers near or far
    So glad as I in thinking?
The gallant world is warm and green,
    For May fulfils November.
When lights and leaves and loves have been,
    Sweet, will you remember?

O star benignant and serene,
   I take the good to-morrow,
That fills from verge to verge my dream,
   With all its joy and sorrow!
The old, sweet spell is unforgot
   That turns to June December;
And, tho' the world remembered not,
   Love, we would remember.

1876

XXIII

THE skies are strown with stars,
    The streets are fresh with dew,
A thin moon drifts to westward,
The night is hushed and cheerful:
    My thought is quick with you.

Near windows gleam and laugh,
    And far away a train
Clanks glowing through the stillness:
A great content's in all things,
    And life is not in vain.

1877

XXIV

THE full sea rolls and thunders
    In glory and in glee.
O bury me not in the senseless earth
    But in the living sea !

Ay, bury me where it surges
    A thousand miles from shore,
And in its brotherly unrest
    I'll range for evermore.

1876

XXV

IN the year that's come and gone love, his flying feather
Stooping slowly, gave us heart, and bade us walk together.
In the year that's coming on though many a troth be broken,
We at least will not forget aught that love hath spoken.

In the year that's come and gone, dear, we wove a tether
All of gracious words and thoughts, binding two together.
In the year that's coming on, with its wealth of roses
We shall weave it stronger yet, ere the circle closes.

In the year that's come and gone, in the golden weather,
Sweet, my sweet, we swore to keep the watch of life together.
In the year that's coming on, rich in joy and sorrow,
We shall light our lamp, and wait life's mysterious morrow.

1877

XXVI

SHE sauntered by the swinging seas;
    A jewel glittered at her ear,
And, teasing her along, the breeze
    Brought many a rounded grace more near.

So passing, one with wave and beam,
    She left for memory to caress
A laughing thought, a golden gleam,
    A hint of hidden loveliness.

1876

XXVII

To S. C.

BLITHE dreams arise to greet us,
    And life feels clean and new,
For the old love comes to meet us
    In the dawning and the dew.
O'erblown with sunny shadows,
    O'ersped with winds at play,
The woodlands and the meadows
    Are keeping holiday.
Wild foals are scampering, neighing—
    Brave merles their hautboys blow.
Come! let us go a-maying
    As in the Long-Ago.

Here we but peak and dwindle:
    The clank of chain and crane,
The whirr of crank and spindle
    Bewilder heart and brain;

The ends of our endeavour
  Are only wealth and fame,
Yet in the still For-Ever
  We're one and all the same;
Delaying, still delaying,
  We watch the fading west;
Come! let us go a-maying,
  Nor fear to take the best.

Yet beautiful and spacious
  The wise old world appears.
Yet frank and fair and gracious
  Outlaugh the jocund years.
Our argument disputing,
  The universal Pan
Still wanders fluting—fluting—
  Fluting to maid and man.
Our weary well-a-waying
  His music cannot still:
Come! let us go a-maying,
  And pipe with him our fill.

Where wanton winds are flowing
    Among the gladdening grass;
Where hawthorn brakes are blowing,
    And meadow perfumes pass;
Where morning's grace is greenest,
    And fullest noon's of pride;
Where sunset spreads serenest,
    And sacred night's most wide;
Where nests are swaying, swaying,
    And spring's fresh voices call,
Come! let us go a-maying,
    And bless the God of all!

1878

XXVIII

To R. L. S.

A CHILD,
  Curious and innocent,
    Slips from his Nurse, and rejoicing
Loses himself in the Fair.

Thro' the jostle and din
Wandering, he revels,
Dreaming, desiring, possessing;
Till, of a sudden
Tired and afraid, he beholds
The sordid assemblage
Just as it is; and he runs
With a sob to his Nurse
(Lighting at last on him)

And in her motherly bosom
Cries him to sleep.

Thus thro' the World,
Seeing and feeling and knowing,
Goes Man, till at last,
Tired of experience, he turns
To the friendly and comforting breast
Of the old nurse, Death.

1876

XXIX

KATE-a-Whimsies, John-a-Dreams,
    Still debating, still delay,
And the world's a ghost that gleams—
    Wavers—vanishes away!

We must live while live we can;
    We should love while love we may.
Dread in woman, doubt in man . . .
    So the Infinite runs away.

1876

XXX

THE pretty washermaiden,
   She washes on always!
And as she rubs, and as she wrings,
Her shapely body sways and springs
   As if to burst her stays.

Her cheek is rich and shining
   And brown as any egg,
And, when she dives into her tub
To duck the linen she's to scrub,
   She shows the neatest leg!

Her round arms white with lather,
   Her elbows fresh and red,
Her mouth the rosiest of buds,
Who would not risk a shower of suds
   To kiss her dainty head?

1876

XXXI

To D. H.

O FALMOUTH is a fine town with ships in the bay,
And I wish from my heart it's there I was to-day;
I wish from my heart I was far away from here,
Sitting in my parlour and talking to my dear.
    For it's home, dearie, home—it's home I want to be.
    Our topsails are hoisted, and we'll away to sea.
    O the oak and the ash and the bonnie birken tree
    They're all growing green in the old countree.

In Baltimore a-walking a lady I did meet
With her babe on her arm as she came down the street;
And I thought how I sailed, and the cradle standing ready
For the pretty little babe that has never seen its daddie.
    And it's home, dearie, home,——

O, if it be a lass, she shall wear a golden ring;
And if it be a lad, he shall fight for his king;
With his dirk and his hat and his little jacket blue
He shall walk the quarter-deck as his daddie used to do.
    And it's home, dearie, home,———

O, there's a wind a-blowing, a-blowing from the west,
And that of all the winds is the one I like the best,
For it blows at our backs, and it shakes our pennon free,
And it soon will blow us home to the old countree.
    For it's home, dearie, home—it's home I want to be.
    Our topsails are hoisted, and we'll away to sea.
    O the oak and the ash and the bonnie birken tree
    They're all growing green in the old countree.

1878

    NOTE.—The burthen and the third stanza are old.

XXXII

THE ways are green with the gladdening sheen
    Of the young year's fairest daughter.
O the shadows that fleet o'er the springing wheat!
    O the magic of running water!
The spirit of spring is in every thing,
    The banners of spring are streaming,
We march to a tune from the fifes of June,
    And life's a dream worth dreaming.

It's all very well to sit and spell
    At the lesson there's no gainsaying;
But what the deuce are wont and use
    When the whole mad world's a-maying?
When the meadow glows, and the orchard snows,
    And the air's with love-motes teeming,
When fancies break, and the senses wake,
    O life's a dream worth dreaming!

What Nature has writ with her lusty wit
    Is worded so wisely and kindly
That whoever has dipped in her manuscript
    Must up and follow her blindly.
Now the summer prime is her blithest rhyme
    In the being and the seeming,
And they that have heard the overword
    Know life's a dream worth dreaming.

1878

XXXIII

To K. de M.

Love blows as the wind blows,
Love blows into the heart.—Nile Boat-Song.

L IFE in her creaking shoes
    Goes, and more formal grows,
A round of calls and cues :
    Love blows as the wind blows.
    Blows ! . . . in the quiet close
As in the roaring mart,
    By ways no mortal knows
Love blows into the heart.

The stars some cadence use,
    Forthright the river flows,
In order fall the dews,
    Love blows as the wind blows.

Blows! . . . and what reckoning shows
The courses of his chart?
A spirit that comes and goes,
Love blows into the heart.

1878

XXXIV

MARGARITÆ SORORI

I. M.

A LATE lark twitters from the quiet skies
 And from the west,
Where the sun, his day's work ended,
Lingers as in content,
There falls on the old, gray city
An influence luminous and serene,
A shining peace.

The smoke ascends
In a rosy-and-golden haze. The spires
Shine, and are changed. In the valley
Shadows rise. The lark sings on. The sun,
Closing his benediction,
Sinks, and the darkening air

Thrills with a sense of the triumphing night—
Night with her train of stars
And her great gift of sleep.

So be my passing!
My task accomplished and the long day done,
My wages taken, and in my heart
Some late lark singing,
Let me be gathered to the quiet west,
The sundown splendid and serene,
Death.

1876

XXXV

OR ever the knightly years were gone
    With the old world to the grave,
I was a king in Babylon
    And you were a christian slave.

I saw, I took, I cast you by,
    I bent and broke your pride.
You loved me well, or I heard them lie,
    But your longing was denied.
Surely I knew that by and by
    You cursed your gods and died.

And a myriad suns have set and shone
    Since then upon the grave
Decreed by the king in Babylon
    To her that had been his slave.

The pride I trampled is now my scathe,
    For it tramples me again.
The old resentment lasts like death,
    For you love, yet you refrain.
I break my heart on your hard unfaith,
    And I break my heart in vain.

Yet not for an hour do I wish undone
    The deed beyond the grave,
When I was a king in Babylon
    And you were a virgin slave.

XXXVI

ON the way to Kew,
    By the river old and gray,
Where in the Long Ago
We laughed and loitered so,
I met a ghost to-day,
A ghost that told of you—
A ghost of low replies
And sweet inscrutable eyes
    Coming up from Richmond
As you used to do.

By the river old and gray,
The enchanted Long Ago
Murmured and smiled anew.
On the way to Kew,

March had the laugh of May,
The bare boughs looked aglow,
And old immortal words
Sang in my breast like birds,
    Coming up from Richmond
As I used with you.

With the life of Long Ago
Lived my thought of you.
By the river old and gray
Flowing his appointed way
As I watched I knew
What is so good to know:
Not in vain, not in vain,
I shall look for you again
    Coming up from Richmond
On the way to Kew.

XXXVII

THE past was goodly once, and yet, when all is said,
The best of it we know is that it's done and dead.

Dwindled and faded quite, perished beyond recall,
Nothing is left at last of what one time was all.

Coming back like a ghost, staring and lingering on,
Never a word it tells but proves it dead and gone.

Duty and work and joy—these things it cannot give;
And the present is life, and life is good to live.

Let it lie where it fell, far from the living sun,
The past that, goodly once, is gone and dead and done.

XXXVIII

THE spring, my dear,
   Is no longer spring.
Does the blackbird sing
What he sang last year?
Are the skies the old
Immemorial blue,
Or am I, or are you,
Grown cold?

Though life be change,
It is hard to bear
When the old sweet air
Sounds forced and strange
To be out of tune,
Plain You and I. . .
It were better to die,
And soon.

XXXIX

To R. A. M. S.

THE Spirit of Wine
    Sang in my glass, and I listened
With love to his odorous music,
His flushed and magnificent song.

——' I am health, I am heart, I am life!
For I give for the asking
The fire of my father the sun,
And the strength of my mother the earth.
Inspiration in essence,
I am wisdom and wit to the wise,
His visible muse to the poet,

The soul of desire to the lover,
The genius of laughter to all.

'Come, lean on me, ye that are weary,
Rise ye faint-hearted and doubting,
Haste ye that lag by the way!
I am pride, the consoler;
Valour and hope are my henchmen;
I am the angel of rest.

'I am life, I am wealth, I am fame:
For I captain an army
Of shining and generous dreams;
And mine, too, all mine, are the keys
Of that secret spiritual shrine,
Where, his work-a-day soul put by,
Shut in with his saint of saints—
With his radiant and conquering self—
Man worships, and talks, and is glad.

'Come, sit with me, ye that are lonely,
Ye that are paid with disdain,

Ye that are chained and would soar!
I am beauty and love;
I am friendship, the comforter;
I am that which forgives and forgets.'——

The Spirit of Wine
Sang in my heart, and I triumphed
In the savour and scent of his music,
His magnetic and mastering song.

XL

A WINK from Hesper falling
   Fast in the wintry sky
Comes through the even blue,
Dear, like a word from you.
   Is it good-bye?

Across the miles between us
   I send you sigh for sigh.
Good-night, sweet friend, good-night:
Till life and all take flight,
   Never good-bye.

XLI

FRIENDS . . old friends . . .
   One sees how it ends.
A woman looks
Or a man tells lies,
And the pleasant brooks
And the quiet skies,
Ruined with brawling
And caterwauling,
Enchant no more
As they did before;
And so it ends
With friends.

Friends . . old friends . . .
And what if it ends?
Shall we dare to shirk
What we live to learn?

It has done its work,
It has served its turn;
And, forgive and forget
Or canker and fret,
We can be no more
As we were before.
When it ends it ends
With friends.

Friends .. old friends ...
So it breaks, so it ends.
There let it rest.
It has fought and won,
And is still the best
That either has done.
Each as he stands
The work of its hands,
Which shall be more
As he was before?
What is it ends
With friends?

XLII

IF it should come to be,
  This proof of you and me,
    This type and sign
Of hours that smiled and shone,
And yet seemed dead and gone
    As old-world wine;

Of Them within the gate
Ask we no richer fate,
    No boon above,
For girl child or for boy,
My gift of life and joy,
    Your gift of love.

XLIII

To W. B. B.

FROM the brake the Nightingale
  Sings exulting to the Rose;
Though he sees her waxing pale
  In her passionate repose,
While she triumphs waxing frail,
  Fading even while she glows;
    Though he knows
    How it goes—
Knows of last year's Nightingale
  Dead with last year's Rose.

Wise the enamoured Nightingale,
  Wise the well-belovèd Rose!
Love and life shall still prevail,
  Nor the silence at the close

Break the magic of the tale
 In the telling, though it shows—
  Who but knows
  How it goes?—
Life a last year's Nightingale,
Love a last year's Rose.

XLIV

MATRI DILECTISSIMÆ

I. M.

IN the waste hour
   Between to-day and yesterday
We watched, while on my arm—
Living flesh of her flesh, bone of her bone—
Dabbled in sweat the sacred head
Lay uncomplaining, still, contemptuous, strange,
Till the dear face turned dead,
And to a sound of lamentation
The good, heroic soul with all its wealth—
Its sixty years of love and sacrifice,
Suffering and passionate faith—was reabsorbed
In the inexorable Peace,
And life was changed to us for evermore.

Was nothing left of her but tears
Like blood-drops from the heart?

Nought save remorse
For duty unfulfilled, justice undone,
And charity ignored? Nothing but love,
Forgiveness, reconcilement, where, in truth,
But for this passing
Into the unimaginable abyss
These things had never been?

Nay, there was we
Her five strong sons.
To her Death came—the great Deliverer came,
As equal comes to equal, throne to throne.
She was a mother of men.

The stars shine as of old, the unchanging river,
Bent on his errand of immortal law,
Works his appointed way
To the immemorial sea;
And the brave truth comes overwhelmingly home,
That she in us yet works and shines,
Lives and fulfils herself,
Unending as the river and the stars.

Dearest, live on
In such an immortality

As we thy sons,
Born of thy body and nursed
At that wild, faithful breast,
Can give—of generous thoughts,
And honourable words, and deeds
That make men half in love with fate.
Live on, O brave and true,
In us thy seed, in ours whose life is thine—
Our best and theirs! What is that best but thou—
Thou, and thy gift to us to pass
Like light along the infinite of space
To the immitigable end?

Between the river and the stars,
O royal and radiant soul,
Thou dost return, thine influences return
Upon thy children as in life, and death
Turns stingless. What is death
But life in act? How should the unteeming grave
Be victor over thee,
Mother, a mother of men?

XLV

CROSSES and troubles a-many have proved me.
    One or two women (God bless them!) have
       loved me.
I have worked and dreamed, and I've talked at will.
Of art and drink I have had my fill.
I've comforted here, and I've succoured there.
I've faced my foes, and I've backed my friends.
I've blundered, and sometimes made amends.
I have prayed for light, and I've known despair.
Now I look before, as I look behind,
Come storm, come shine, whatever befall,
With a grateful heart and a constant mind,
For the end I know is the best of all.

BRIC-À-BRAC

BALLADES
RONDELS
SONNETS AND QUATORZAINS
RONDEAUS

'*The tune of the time.*'—HAMLET, *concerning* OSRIC.

BALLADES

OF A TOYOKUNI COLOUR-PRINT

To W. A.

WAS I a Samurai renowned,
    Two-sworded, fierce, immense of bow?
A histrion angular and profound?
A priest? a porter?—Child, although
I have forgotten clean, I know
That in the shade of Fujisan,
What time the cherry-orchards blow,
I loved you once in old Japan.

As here you loiter, flowing-gowned
And hugely sashed, with pins a-row
Your quaint head as with flamelets crowned,
Demure, inviting—even so,

When merry maids in Miyako
To feel the sweet o' the year began,
And green gardens to overflow,
I loved you once in old Japan.

Clear shine the hills; the rice-fields round
Two cranes are circling; sleepy and slow,
A blue canal the lake's blue bound
Breaks at the bamboo bridge; and lo!
Touched with the sundown's spirit and glow,
I see you turn, with flirted fan,
Against the plum-tree's bloomy snow. . . .
I loved you once in old Japan!

Envoy

Dear, 'twas a dozen lives ago;
But that I was a lucky man
The Toyokuni here will show:
I loved you—once—in old Japan.

OF YOUTH AND AGE

To T. E. B.

SPRING at her height on a morn at prime,
    Sails that laugh from a flying squall,
Pomp of harmony, rapture of rhyme—
Youth is the sign of them one and all.
Winter sunsets and leaves that fall,
An empty flagon, a folded page,
A tumble-down wheel, a tattered ball—
These are a type of the world of Age.

Bells that clash in a gaudy chime,
Swords that clatter in onsets tall,
The words that ring and the fames that climb—
Youth is the sign of them one and all.
Hymnals old in a dusty stall,
A bald, blind bird in a crazy cage,
The scene of a faded festival—
These are a type of the world of Age.

Hours that strut as the heirs of time,
Deeds whose rumour's a clarion-call,
Songs where the singers their souls sublime—
Youth is the sign of them one and all.
A staff that rests in a nook of wall,
A reeling battle, a rusted gage,
The chant of a nearing funeral—
These are a type of the world of Age.

Envoy

Struggle and turmoil, revel and brawl—
Youth is the sign of them, one and all.
A smouldering hearth and a silent stage—
These are a type of the world of Age.

OF THE FROWARDNESS OF WOMAN

To E. S.

ALL the idols are overthrowing,
　Man the end of his reign descries.
Maids are clamouring, wives are crowing,
Widows thrill with a wild surmise.
Those one follows and those one flies,
The loth to be won and the willing to woo,
Look at the world with longing eyes.
Nothing is left for the men to do.

Pulpit and platform overflowing,
Ready the scheme of things to revise,
See them—eager, militant, knowing—
Write, plead, wrangle, philologize,
Answer papers, and vote supplies,
Wield a racquet, handle a cue,
Paint, fight, legislate, theorize.
Nothing is left for the men to do.

Cora's riding and Lilian's rowing,
Celia's novels are books one buys,
Julia's lecturing, Phyllis is mowing,
Sue is a dealer in oils and dyes,
Flora and Dora poetize,
Jane's a bore and Bee is a blue,
Sylvia lives to anatomize.
Nothing is left for the men to do.

Envoy

Prince, our past on the dust-heap lies!
Saving to scrub, to bake, to brew,
Nurse, dress, prattle, and scandalize,
Nothing is left for the men to do.

OF RAIN

To H. W.

A SOMBRE, sagging sky
  Of tossed and tumbled wrack
And ragged clouds that lie
To meet the wind's attack,
Or march in columns black
And serried; then a still,
A feverish kind of thrill;
And whispering in the leaves,
And pattering on the pane,
It falls in very sheaves,
The weary dreary rain.

The summer seems to sigh
As she were flouted back.

The grasses rot and die,
The corn begins to crack.
The flowers would like to pack,
It's all so dank and chill,
Discomfortable and shrill:
While, flickering from the eaves
And gurgling down the drain,
The sodden world receives
The weary, dreary rain.

The big trees, broad and high,
Grow thick and blurred and slack.
The birds, too dull to fly,
Brood dismal, and the track
Shines. If a sudden quack
Sound from the ducks that swill,
The damp hush takes it ill.
But ever and on it weaves
Its rhythms with might and main,
And all its will achieves,
The weary, dreary rain.

Envoy

It lapses not: it cleaves
A way to heart and brain;
It dins, it duns, it deaves,
It worries and wastes and grieves,
The weary, dreary rain.

OF ANTIQUE DANCES

To A. D.

BEFORE the town had lost its wits,
    And scared the bravery from its beaux,
When money-grubs were merely cits,
And verse was crisp and clear as prose,
Ere Chloë and Strephon came to blows
For votes, degrees, and cigarettes,
The world rejoiced to point its toes
In Gigues, Gavottes, and Minuets.

The solemn fiddlers touch their kits;
The tinkling clavichord o'erflows
With contrapuntal quirks and hits;
And, with all measure and repose,
Through figures grave as royal shows,
With noble airs and pirouettes,
They move, to rhythms HANDEL knows,
In Gigues, Gavottes, and Minuets.

O Fans and Swords, O Sacques and Mits,
That was the better part you chose!
You know not how those gamesome chits,
Waltz, Polka, and Schottische, arose,
Nor how Quadrille—a kind of doze
In time and tune—the dance besets;
You aired your fashion to the close
In Gigues, Gavottes, and Minuets.

Envoy

Muse of the many-twinkling hose,
TERPSICHORE, O teach your pets
The charm that shines, the grace that glows
In Gigues, Gavottes, and Minuets.

OF SPRING MUSIC

To W. H. P.

SOUNDS of waking, sounds of growing
　　Seem the living air to fill.
Hark! the echoes are yeo-hoing
Valiantly from vale and hill!
Nature's voices, moving still
In a larger, lustier swing,
Work together with a will.
'Tis the symphony of Spring!

Showers are singing, clouds are flowing,
Ocean thunders, croons the rill.
Hark! the West his clarion's blowing!
Hark! the thrush is fluting shrill,
And the blackbird tries his trill,
And the skylark soars to sing!
Even the sparrow tunes his quill.
'Tis the symphony of Spring!

Lambs are bleating, steers are lowing,
Brisk and rhythmic clacks the mill.
Kapellmeister April, glowing
And superb with glee and skill,
Comes, his orchestra to drill
In a music that will ring
Till the gray world yearn and thrill:
'Tis the symphony of Spring!

Envoy

Princes, though your blood be chill,
Here's shall make you leap and fling,
Fling and leap like Jack and Jill!
'Tis the symphony of Spring.

OF MIDSUMMER DAYS AND NIGHTS

To W. H.

WITH a ripple of leaves and a tinkle of streams
The full world rolls in a rhythm of praise,
And the winds are one with the clouds and beams—
Midsummer days! midsummer days!
The dusk grows vast; in a purple haze,
While the West from a rapture of sunset rights,
Faint stars their exquisite lamps upraise—
Midsummer nights! O midsummer nights!

The wood's green heart is a nest of dreams,
The lush grass thickens and springs and sways,
The rathe wheat rustles, the landscape gleams—
Midsummer days! midsummer days!
In the stilly fields, in the stilly ways,
All secret shadows and mystic lights,
Late lovers murmur and linger and gaze—
Midsummer nights! O midsummer nights!

There's a music of bells from the trampling teams,
Wild skylarks hover, the gorses blaze,
The rich, ripe rose as with incense steams—
Midsummer days! midsummer days!
A soul from the honeysuckle strays,
And the nightingale as from prophet heights
Sings to the Earth of her million Mays—
Midsummer nights! O midsummer nights!

Envoy

And it's O for my dear and the charm that stays—
Midsummer days! midsummer days!
It's O for my Love and the dark that plights—
Midsummer nights! O midsummer nights!

OF DEAD ACTORS

To E. J. H.

WHERE are the passions they essayed,
    And where the tears they made to flow?
Where the wild humours they portrayed
For laughing worlds to see and know?
Othello's wrath and Juliet's woe?
Sir Peter's whims and Timon's gall?
And Millamant and Romeo?
Into the night go one and all.

Where are the braveries, fresh or frayed?
The plumes the armours—friend and foe?
The cloth of gold, the rare brocade,
The mantles glittering to and fro?
The pomp, the pride, the royal show?
The cries of war and festival?
The youth, the grace, the charm, the glow?
Into the night go one and all.

The curtain falls, the play is played:
The Beggar packs beside the Beau;
The Monarch troops, and troops the Maid;
The Thunder huddles with the Snow.
Where are the revellers high and low?
The clashing swords? The lover's call?
The dancers gleaming row on row?
Into the night go one and all.

Envoy

Prince, in one common overthrow
The Hero tumbles with the Thrall:
As dust that drives, as straws that blow,
Into the night go one and all.

MADE IN THE HOT WEATHER

To C. M.

FOUNTAINS that frisk and sprinkle
　　The moss they overspill;
Pools that the breezes crinkle;
　　The wheel beside the mill,
　　With its wet, weedy frill;
Wind-shadows in the wheat;
　　A water-cart in the street;
The fringe of foam that girds
　　An islet's ferneries;
A green sky's minor thirds—
　　To live, I think of these!

Of ice and glass the tinkle,
　　Pellucid, silver-shrill,

Peaches without a wrinkle;
Cherries and snow at will
From china bowls that fill
The senses with a sweet
Incuriousness of heat;
A melon's dripping sherds;
Cream-clotted strawberries;
Dusk dairies set with curds—
To live, I think of these!

Vale-lily and periwinkle;
Wet stone-crop on the sill;
The look of leaves a-twinkle
With windlets clear and still;
The feel of a forest rill
That wimples fresh and fleet
About one's naked feet;
The muzzles of drinking herds;
Lush flags and bulrushes;
The chirp of rain-bound birds—
To live, I think of these!

Envoy

Dark aisles, new packs of cards,
Mermaidens' tails, cool swards,
Dawn dews and starlit seas,
White marbles, whiter words —
To live, I think of these!

OF JUNE

To W. W.

LILACS glow, and jasmines climb,
　　Larks are loud the livelong day.
O the golden summer-prime!
June takes up the sceptre of May,
And the land beneath her sway
Blooms, a dream of blossoming closes,
And the very wind's at play
With Sir Love among the roses.

Lights and shadows in the lime
Meet in exquisite disarray.
Hark! the rich recurrent rhyme
Of the blackbird's roundelay!
Where he carols frank and gay
Fancy no more glooms nor proses:
Joyously she trips away
With Sir Love among the roses.

O the cool sea's slumbrcus chime!
O the links that beach the bay
Paven with meadow-sweet and thyme
Where the brown bees murmur and stray!
Lush the hedgerows, ripe the hay,
Many a maiden, binding posies,
Finds herself at Yea-and-Nay
With Sir Love among the roses.

Envoy

Boys and girls, be wise, I pray:
Do as dear Queen June proposes,
For she bids you troop and stay
With Sir Love among the roses.

OF LADIES' NAMES

To A. L.

BROWN is for Lalage, Jones for Lelia,
  Robinson's bosom for Beatrice glows,
Smith is a Hamlet before Ophelia.
The glamour stays if the reason goes:
Every lover the years disclose
Is of a beautiful name made free.
One befriends, and all others are foes:
Anna's the name of names for me.

Sentiment hallows the vowels of Delia;
Sweet simplicity breathes from Rose!
Courtly memories glitter in Celia;
Rosalind savours of quips and hose,
Araminta of wits and beaux,
Prue of puddings, and Coralie
All of sawdust and spangled shows:
Anna's the name of names for me.

Fie upon Caroline, Jane, Amelia—
These I reckon the essence of prose !—
Mystical Magdalen, cold Cornelia,
Adelaide's attitudes, Mopsa's mowes,
Maud's magnificence, Totty's toes,
Poll and Bet with their twang of the sea,
Nell's impertinence, Pamela's woes !
Anna's the name of names for me.

Envoy

Ruth like a gillyflower smells and blows,
Sylvia prattles of Arcady,
Portia's only a Roman nose,
Anna's the name of names for me.

OF LIFE AND FATE

To T. G. H.

FOOLS may pine, and sots may swill,
    Cynics gibe and prophets rail,
Moralists may scourge and drill,
Preachers prose, and fainthearts quail.
Let them whine, or threat, or wail!
Till the touch of Circumstance
Down to darkness sink the scale,
Fate's a fiddler, Life's a dance.

What if skies be wan and chill?
What if winds be harsh and stale?
Presently the east will thrill,
And the sad and shrunken sail,
Bellying with a kindly gale,
Bear you sunwards, while your chance
Sends you back the hopeful hail,
'Fate's a fiddler, Life's a dance.'

Idle shot or coming bill,
Hapless love or broken bail,
Gulp it (never chew your pill!),
And if Burgundy should fail,
Try a humble pot of ale!
Over all is heaven's expanse.
Gold exists among the shale.
Fate's a fiddler, Life's a dance.

Dull Sir Joskin sleeps his fill,
Good Sir Galahad seeks the Grail,
Proud Sir Pertinax flaunts his frill,
Hard Sir Æger dints his mail;
And the while by hill and dale
Tristram's braveries gleam and glance,
And his blithe horn tells its tale,
'Fate's a fiddler, Life's a dance.'

Araminta's grand and shrill,
Delia's passionate and frail,
Doris drives an earnest quill,
Athanasia takes the veil

Wiser Phyllis o'er her pail,
At the heart of all romance
Reading, sings to Strephon's flail,
'Fate's a fiddler, Life's a dance.'

Every Jack must have his Jill,
(Even Johnson had his Thrale!)
Forward, couples—with a will!
This, the world, is not a jail.
Hear the music, sprat and whale!
Hands across, retire, advance!
Though the doomsman's on your trail,
Fate's a fiddler, Life's a dance.

Envoy

Boys and girls, at slug and snail
And their kindred look askance.
Pay your footing on the nail:
Fate's a fiddler, Life's a dance.

RONDELS

I

'Por la calle de Despues se acabe à la casa de Nunca'

IN the street of By-and-By
   Stands the hostelry of Never.
Dream from deed he must dissever
Who his fortune here would try.

There's a pathos in the cry,
As of impotent endeavour:
In the street of By-and-By
Stands the hostelry of Never.

Grave or gamesome, low or high,
Dull or dainty, crass or clever,
You must lose your chance for ever,
If you let it forth to fly
In the street of By-and-By.

II

'Hic habitat Felicitas'

'FELICITY. Enquire within.
　　Truly the goddess is at home!'
So read, so thought, the rakes of Rome,
Some frail one's lintel fain to win.

And now it blares thro' bronze and tin,
Thro' clarion, organ, catcall, comb:
'Felicity. Enquire within.
Truly the goddess is at home!'

For, tent or studio, bank or bin,
Platonic porch, Petræan dome,
Where'er our hobbies champ and foam,
Thereo'er the brave old sign we pin:
'Felicity. Enquire within.'

III

'Alons au bois le may cueillir'—CHARLES D'ORLÉANS.

WE'll to the woods and gather may
    Fresh from the footprints of the rain.
We'll to the woods, at every vein
To drink the spirit of the day.

The winds of spring are out at play,
The needs of spring in heart and brain.
We'll to the woods and gather may
Fresh from the footprints of the rain.

The world's too near her end, you say?
Hark to the blackbird's mad refrain!
It waits for her, the vast Inane?
Then, girls, to help her on the way
We'll to the woods and gather may.

IV

BESIDE the idle summer sea
    And in the vacant summer days
Light Love came fluting down the ways
Where you were loitering with me.

Who has not welcomed even as we
That jocund minstrel and his lays
Beside the idle summer sea
And in the vacant summer days?

We listened, we were fancy-free;
And lo! in terror and amaze
We stood alone—alone at gaze
With an implacable memory
Beside the idle summer sea.

V

R. G. C. B.

MDCCCLXXVIII

I. M.

THE ways of Death are soothing and serene,
    And all the words of Death are grave and sweet.
From camp and church, the fireside and the street,
She beckons forth—and strife and song have been.

A summer night descending cool and green
And dark on daytime's dust and stress and heat,
The ways of Death are soothing and serene,
And all the words of Death are grave and sweet.

O glad and sorrowful, with triumphant mien
And radiant faces look upon and greet
This last of all your lovers, and to meet
Her kiss, the Comforter's, your spirit lean. . . .
The ways of Death are soothing and serene.

VI

WE shall surely die:
    Must we needs grow old?
Grow old and cold,
And we know not why?

O the By-and-By,
And the tale that's told!
We shall surely die:
Must we needs grow old?

Grow old and sigh,
Grudge and withhold,
Resent and scold? . . .
Not you and I?
We shall surely die!

SONNETS AND QUATORZAINS

AT QUEENSFERRY

To W. G. S.

THE blackbird sang, the skies were clear and clean.
   We bowled along a road that curved its spine
Superbly sinuous and serpentine
Thro' silent symphonies of summer green.
Sudden the Forth came on us—sad of mien,
No cloud to colour it, no breeze to line:
A sheet of dark, dull glass, without a sign
Of life or death, two beams of sand between.
Water and sky merged blank in mist together,
The fort loomed spectral, and the guardship's spars
Traced vague, black shadows on the shimmery glaze:
We felt the dim strange years, the gray strange weather,
The still strange land, unvexed of sun or stars,
Where Lancelot rides clanking thro' the haze.

ORIENTALE

SHE's an enchanting little Israelite,
    A world of hidden dimples!—dusky-eyed,
A starry-glancing daughter of the Bride,
With hair escaped from some Arabian Night,
Her lip is red, her cheek is golden-white,
Her nose a scimitar; and, set aside
The bamboo hat she cocks with so much pride,
Her dress a dream of daintiness and delight.
And when she passes with the dreadful boys
And romping girls, the cockneys loud and crude,
My thought, to the Minories tied yet moved to range
The land o' the sun, commingles with the noise
Of magian drums and scents of sandalwood
A touch Sidonian—modern—brilliant—strange!

FORENOON

SOFT as the whisper shut within a shell,
　　The far sea rustles white along the sand,
A tiny breeze, blown wanton from the land,
Teases it into dimples visible ;
A dream of blue, the Fife hills sink and swell ;
The large light quivers, and from strand to strand
A vast content seems breathing to expand ;
And the deep heaven smiles down a sleepy spell.
Dark bathers bob ; the girders of the pier
Stand softened forth against the quiet blue ;
Dogs bark ; the wading children take their pleasure ;
A horse comes charging round, and I can hear
The gallop's wild waltz-rhythm, falling thro',
Change to the trot's deliberate polka-measure.

IN FISHERROW

A HARD north-easter fifty winters long
　　Has bronzed and shrivelled sere her face and neck;
Her locks are wild and gray, her teeth a wreck;
Her foot is vast, her bowed leg spare and strong.
A wide blue cloak, a squat and sturdy throng
Of curt blue coats, a mutch without a speck,
A white vest broidered black, her person deck,
Nor seems their stern and old-world quaintness wrong.
Her great creel forehead-slung, she wanders nigh,
Easing the heavy strap with gnarled, brown fingers,
The spirit of commerce watchful in her eye,
Ever and anon imploring you to buy,
As looking down the street she onward lingers,
Reproachful, with a strange and doleful eye.

RAIN

THE sky saggs low with convoluted cloud,
    Heavy and imminent, rolled from rim to rim.
A bank of fog blots out of sight the brim
Of the leaden sea, all spiritless and cowed.
The rain is falling sheer and strong and loud,
The strand is desolate, the distance grim
With threats of storm, the wet stones glimmer dim,
And to the wall the dank umbrellas crowd.
At home . . . the dank shrubs whisper dismal mooded,
Black chimney-shadows streak the shiny slates,
The eaves are strung with drops, and steeped the
    grasses,
A draggled fishwife screeches at the gates,
The baker hurries dripping on, and hooded
In her wet prints a pretty housemaid passes.

BACK-VIEW

To D. F.

I WATCHED you saunter down the sand :
   Serene and large, the golden weather
Flowed radiant round your peacock feather,
And glistered from your jewelled hand.
Your tawny hair, turned strand on strand
And bound with ribands blue together,
Streaked the rough tartan, green like heather,
That round your lissome shoulder spanned.
Your grace was quick my sense to seize :
The quaint looped hat, the twisted tresses,
The close-drawn scarf, and under these
The flowing, flapping draperies—
My thought an outline still caresses,
Enchanting, comic, Japanese!

CROQUIS

To G. W.

THE beach was crowded. Pausing now and then,
  He groped and fiddled doggedly along,
His worn face glaring on the thoughtless throng
The stony peevishness of sightless men.
He seemed scarce older than his clothes. Again,
Grotesquing thinly many an old sweet song,
So cracked his viol, his hand so frail and wrong,
You hardly could distinguish one in ten.
He stopped at last, and sate him on the sand,
And, grasping wearily his bread-winner,
Stared dim towards the blue immensity,
Then leaned his head upon his poor old hand.
He may have slept: he did not speak nor stir:
His gesture spoke a vast despondency.

JENNY WREN

MISS WREN is O so wee, so wee!
   So light, so light! So neat, so neat!
Her waist is trig as waist can be.
She has the funniest little feet,
The prettiest hands, the sauciest nose,
The blackest eyes, the reddest lips!
She comes, she looks, she laughs, she goes,
With petulant little turns and dips.
Her little self she perks and plumes.
She chirps and twitters, chirps and cheeps
As though among wet apple-blooms,
With sudden, sidelong, little leaps,
She flits, she flies! Was never seen
A daintier little cutty-quean.

ATTADALE WEST HIGHLANDS

To A. J.

A BLACK and glassy float, opaque and still,
　　The loch, at furthest ebb supine in sleep,
Reversing, mirrored in its luminous deep
The calm gray skies; the solemn spurs of hill;
Heather and corn and wisps of loitering haze;
The wee white cots, black-hatted, plumed with smoke;
The braes beyond—and when the ripple awoke,
They wavered with the jarred and wavering glaze.
The air was hushed and dreamy. Evermore
A noise of running water whispered near.
A straggling crow cawed high and thin. A bird
Trilled from the birch-leaves. Round the shingled shore,
Yellow with weed, there wandered, vague and clear,
Strange vowels, mysterious gutturals, idly heard.

FROM A WINDOW IN PRINCES STREET

To M. M. M'B.

ABOVE the Crags that fade and gloom
    Starts the bare knee of Arthur's Seat;
Ridged high against the evening bloom,
The Old Town rises, street on street;
With lamps bejewelled, straight ahead,
Like rampired walls the houses lean,
All spired and domed and turreted,
Sheer to the valley's darkling green;
Ranged in mysterious disarray,
The Castle, menacing and austere,
Looms through the lingering last of day;
And in the silver dusk you hear,
Reverberated from crag and scar,
Bold bugles blowing points of war.

IN THE DIALS

TO *Garryowen* upon an organ ground
    Two girls are jigging. Riotously they trip,
With eyes aflame, quick bosoms, hand on hip,
As in the tumult of a witches' round.
A crowd of youngsters round them prance and bound,
Two solemn babes twirl ponderously, and skip.
The artist's teeth gleam from his bearded lip.
High from the kennel yells a tortured hound.
The music reels and hurtles, and the night
Is full of stinks and cries; a naphtha light
Flares from a barrow; battered and obtused
With vices, wrinkles, life and work and rags,
Each with her inch of clay, two loitering hags
Look on dispassionate—critical—something mused.

RONDEAUS

I

MY love to me is always kind:
   She neither storms, nor is she pined;
She does not plead with tears or sighs,
But gentle words and soft replies—
Good earnest of the thought behind.

They say the little god is blind,
They do not count him quite too wise;
Yet he, somehow, could bring and bind
              My love to me.

And sweetest nut hath sourest rind?
It may be so; but she I prize
Is even lovelier in mine eyes
Than good and gracious to my mind.
I bless the fortune that consigned
              My love to me.

II

WITH strawberries we filled a tray,
    And then we drove away, away
Along the links beside the sea,
Where wave and wind were light and free,
And August felt as fresh as May.

And where the springy turf was gay
With thyme and balm and many a spray
Of wild roses, you tempted me
    With strawberries.

A shadowy sail, silent and gray,
Stole like a ghost across the bay;
But none could hear me ask my fee,
And none could know what came to be.
Can sweethearts *all* their thirst allay
    With strawberries?

III

THE leaves are sere, and on the ground
    They rustle with an eerie sound,
A sound half-whisper and half-sigh—
The plaint of sweet things fain to die,
Sad things for which no ruth is found.

With summer once the land was crowned;
But now that autumn scatters round
Decay, and summer fancies die,
        The leaves are sere.

Once, too, my thought within the bound
Of summer frolicked, like a hound
In meadows jocund with July.
Yet now I sit and wonder why,
With all my waste of penny and pound,
        The leaves are sere.

IV

To F. W.

LET us be drunk, and for a while forget,
    Forget and, ceasing even from regret,
Live without reason and in spite of rhyme,
As in a dream preposterous and sublime,
Where place and hour and means for once are met.

Where is the use of effort? Love and debt
And disappointment have us in a net.
Let us break out, and taste the morning's prime . . .
    Let us be drunk.

In vain our little hour we strut and fret,
And mouth our wretched parts as for a bet:
We cannot please the tragicaster Time.
To gain the crystal sphere, the silver clime,
Where Sympathy sits dimpling on us yet
    Let us be drunk!

V

To H. D. C.

IF I were king my pipe should be premier.
 The skies of time and chance are seldom clear;
We would inform them all with azure weather.
Delight alone would need to shed a tear,
For dream and deed should war no more together.

Art should aspire, yet ugliness be dear;
Beauty, the shaft, should speed with wit for feather;
And love, sweet love, should never fall to sere
          If I were king.

But politics should find no harbour near;
The Philistine should dread to slip his tether;
Tobacco should be duty free, and beer;
In fact, in room of this the age of leather,
An age of gold all radiant should appear
          If I were king.

VI

WHEN you are old, and I am passed away—
    Passed, and your face, your golden face, is gray—
I think, whate'er the end, this dream of mine,
Comforting you, a friendly star will shine
Down the dim slope where still you stumble and stray.

So may it be : that so dead Yesterday,
No sad-eyed ghost but generous and gay,
May serve you memories like almighty wine,
    When you are old.

Dear Heart, it shall be so. Under the sway
Of death the past's enormous disarray

Lies hushed and dark. Yet though there come no sign,
Live on well pleased : immortal and divine
Love shall still tend you, as God's angels may,
   When you are old.

VII

WHAT is to come we know not. But we know
    That what has been was good—was good to
        show,
Better to hide, and best of all to bear.
We are the masters of the days that were.
We have lived, we have loved, we have suffered . . .
        even so.

Shall we not take the ebb who had the flow?
Life was our friend. Now, if it be our foe—
Dear, though it spoil and break us!—need we care
        What is to come?

Let the great winds their worst and wildest blow,
Or the gold weather round us mellow slow;

We have fulfilled ourselves, and we can dare
And we can conquer, though we may not share
In the rich quiet of the afterglow
                What is to come.

CPSIA information can be obtained
at www.ICGtesting.com
Printed in the USA
LVHW091352061120
670962LV00001B/27